REBUN IS.
RISITIRI IS.

SEA OF OKHOTSK

DAISETSUZAN
MT. AKAN
L. AKAN

Sapporo

HOKKAIDO

Kushiro   Nemuro

Hakodate

TUNNEL

Akita

PACIFIC
OCEAN

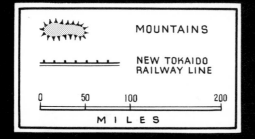

	MOUNTAINS
	NEW TOKAIDO RAILWAY LINE

0   50   100   200

M I L E S

ndai

Population (July 1967) Over 100,000,000. Japan is the seventh country in the world with a population of more than 100,000,000 —after China, India, the U.S.S.R., the U.S.A., Indonesia and Pakistan. As Japan is so mountainous most of the huge industrial cities are crowded together on the plains.

Population of largest cities

Tokyo	10,870,000
Osaka	3,150,000
Nagoya	1,930,000
Yokohama	1,790,000
Kyoto	1,360,000
Kobe	1,210,000
Kitayushu	1,040,000

Name The Japanese call their country Nippon or Nihon which means "the sunrise". Our word Japan comes from the name "Jipangu". This is what the Venetian explorer Marco Polo called the islands when he travelled through China in the thirteenth century.

Calendar In 1968 the emperor was in the forty-third year of his reign which is called *Showa*. In the Japanese calendar 1968 is *Showa* 43. Years are named after the twelve animals of the zodiac (a Chinese custom). 1968 was the "Year of the Monkey".

Forms of Address The Japanese bow instead of shaking hands when greeting. On formal occasions, for example when greeting friends in the home, it is the custom to kneel, place the palms of the hands on the floor and make a deep bow, the forehead almost touching the back of the hands. When the Japanese wish to be very polite —such as when children address their grandparents—they use the extra word "o", which means noble. *Cha* is the word for tea, but at a tea ceremony it would be called *o-cha*, noble tea.

Some Facts and Figures

Area 142,726 square miles. Of this, only 15 per cent is agricultural land ; the remainder is made up of mountains, forests and lakes.

The country's three most important industrial districts are :
the plain around Tokyo and Yokohama— the district surrounding Nagoya and Kyoto—along the shores of the Inland Sea (particularly around Osaka and Kobe). Seventy per cent of Japan's industry is in these districts, and 80 per cent of Honshu's population lives here.

Looking at JAPAN

In Japan a seal is used where a signature would be
used in other countries—on letters and receipts,
and for cashing cheques and postal orders.
This is the author's seal

Looking at

GWYNNETH ASHBY

Adam and Charles Black   London

J. B. Lippincott Company   Philadelphia and New York

Rice paddies

JAPAN

Looking at Other Countries

Looking at HOLLAND   **Looking at NORWAY**

Looking at ITALY   **Looking at DENMARK**

Looking at GREECE   **Looking at JAPAN**

Further titles in preparation

I should like to express my appreciation for the help and
hospitality I received when in Japan. In particular I should like
to thank Yoshinao Odaka and the staff of the Overseas Public
Relations Section, Ministry of Foreign Affairs; the staffs of the
Tourist Offices, both in London and Japan, and of the Japan
Information Centre in London; Ayuchi Takita of Japan Air Lines,
Tokyo; T. J. Adkin; Reitaro Fujita of Kyoto; Hiromi Ikeda of
Marugame, Joichi Ninomiya of Matsuyama, and Tsuyoshi Araki
of Nagasaki. My special thanks are due to the Sudo family who
gave me hospitality at their home in Tokyo. I am also most
grateful to Japan Air Lines for their assistance.   GA

Acknowledgement is due to the following for their permission to
reproduce photographs:
Associated Press 13b
Ehime Prefecture office 28, 52
Hideo Yoshikawa 48b
Hidetoshi Shimane 17a, 56
Japan Air Lines cover a, 61
Japan Information Centre, London 5, 9a, 10, 14a and b, 16b,
17b and c, 25, 29b, 32, 40b, 48c
Japan Silk Association Inc 53b
Koshi Akeda 29a
Mary Ramirez 24b, 57b
Overseas Public Relations Section, Ministry of Foreign Affairs,
Tokyo 8, 9b, 20, 21a, 33, 36a and b, 37, 40a, 41, 42a, 44a, 45,
48a, 49a and b, 53a, 57a, 59a, 60a and b
The Trustees of the British Museum 11, 12a, 22
T. J. Adkin 13a, 16a, 17d, 24a, 44b, 49c

Apart from the above all the photographs are by the author

The map and drawings are by H. Johns

CONTENTS

The unit of
currency is
the *yen*.
(£1=860 yen,
$1=360 yen)

The Country

Torii at Miyajima, an island in the Inland Sea —there is a *torii* at the entrance to every Shinto shrine

This old archway is as much a part of Japan as the transistor radios and clicking cameras which are found everywhere. Japan is a country of old and new, with children in Western clothes and priests in ancient robes, with modern industries and ancient shrines.

The land of Japan also has its contrasts. On the plains there are large cities with concrete buildings and factories, and crowds of people; while in the mountains, which cover four-fifths of Japan, the scenery includes active volcanoes and pools of boiling mud, emerald-green lakes fed by mountain snows, groves of bamboo and forests of cedar and maple. The Japan Alps in central Honshu have more than a dozen peaks over 8000 feet, and to the south the country's highest peak, Fuji-san, reaches 12,388 feet. In spring people go into the country in thousands to see the cherry blossom, and in autumn to enjoy chrysanthemums, and hillsides aflame with maples.

6

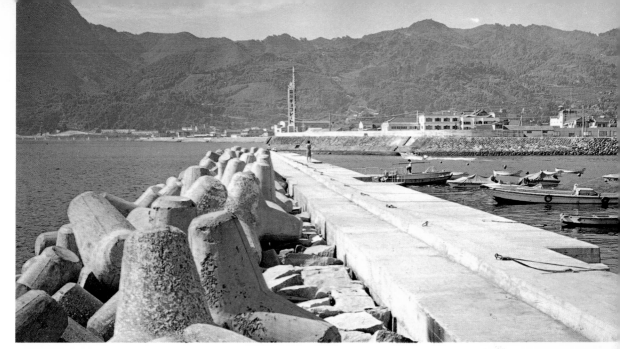

Japan is made up of a group of islands which stretch for about 1600 miles in the North Pacific. There are four main islands—Hokkaido, Honshu, Shikoku and Kyushu—as well as hundreds of smaller ones. The capital, Tokyo, and most of the important towns are on Honshu, which is almost the same size as Great Britain.

Typhoon boulders

As the islands stretch so far from north to south the climate varies from the cold winters and heavy snowfalls of Hokkaido to the sticky subtropical climate of the Ryukyu islands in the south. There is a rainy season in June, and between late August and October typhoons bring heavy rainfall. These typhoons sometimes sweep away roads and bridges, break river banks and disrupt telephone and electricity services.

Cities and villages are cut off by raging flood waters, and houses crushed by landslides. On some coasts special "typhoon boulders" are placed along the sea wall to break the force of the waves. Japan has many small earth tremors, and occasionally there is an earthquake which wrecks hundreds of homes.

History

Burning the grass on Mt. Wakakusa—
this ancient festival is held annually in Nara to
mark the ending of a quarrel between two temples

Drops of water falling from the sword of a heavenly deity and forming islands—this, say the ancient legends, was how Japan began. The two deities who lived on the islands had a daughter whose great-grandson Jimmu became the first emperor of Japan in 660 B C.

For hundreds of years many Japanese believed in the divine birth of Jimmu and that every emperor was directly descended from him. But after the Second World War the present emperor, Hirohito, made a speech over the radio declaring that he was not a god, but an ordinary human being.

8

Prince
Shotoku

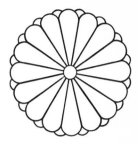

Imperial crest

At the beginning of the fourth century a number of family clans were joined into the state of Yamato. The leaders of the Yamato court are probably the real ancestors of the Japanese Imperial Family.

One of Japan's best known historical figures was Prince Shotoku (AD 573–621) who acted as regent for his mother. He encouraged the new religion of Buddhism, and brought in experts to teach new ways of weaving and farming. Many beautiful and useful articles—mirrors and lacquer work, writing materials, silks and glass —were introduced into the country from the mainland.

During the eighth and ninth centuries, new capitals were built at Nara and Kyoto. In this period the Fujiwaras rose to power. For over 300 years they were the real rulers of Japan, while the emperors, who were considered too sacred to be seen by the ordinary people, occupied themselves with the life of the court and religious ceremonies.

The great image of Buddha at Nara

9

The Fujiwaras so enjoyed living in the capital of Kyoto, that they neglected the provinces, and fighting broke out between the different clans. In 1192 Yoritomo of the Minamoto clan took the title of *shogun*, military dictator. (Japan was ruled by military governments until 1868.)

Yoritomo made Kamakura, a fishing village near the modern port of Yokohama, his capital. During the Kamakura period (1185–1333) feudalism started to develop. (Feudalism was a system by which men fought for their lord in return for his protection and the right to farm his land.) Everyone belonged to a certain class and it was almost impossible to better oneself. At the top there was the *shogun* and his *daimyo* (lords), followed by the *samurai* (lords' retainers), then there were the farmers and craftsmen, and the merchants and moneylenders.

In the Muromachi period (1336–1573) which followed, Kyoto became the capital again, and there were many fights between

Scene from
a *Noh* play

東海道
五拾三次
之内

日本橋

Woodblock print by
Hiroshige

the different clans. Then, in the sixteenth and early seventeenth centuries three great military leaders welded the clans
into one nation. In 1603 Ieyasu of the Tokugawa clan became
the first Tokugawa *shogun*, and for over 200 years his descend-
ants ruled the country.

In the 1540's Portuguese merchants arrived with clocks and
spectacles, leather and velvet goods, Arab horses and guns.
Missionaries introduced Christianity and new ideas—the
theory that the world is round, and knowledge of comets and
astronomy. Then, in the 1630's the government forbade
Christianity and allowed no foreigners into Japan. They were
afraid that the new ideas would cause unrest. Anyone who
tried to leave, or enter (even if shipwrecked), was put to death.
During this "closed" period the only people allowed to stay
and trade in Japan were a few Dutch and Chinese, and they
had to live on a small island near Nagasaki.

Perry arriving in Tokyo Bay

In 1853 an American naval force commanded by Commodore Perry anchored in Tokyo Bay bringing a demand from President Fillmore that Japan should open her ports to world trade. Japan agreed, and within a few years treaties were signed with Great Britain, the Netherlands, Russia and France.

At this time Japan had no trains or steamships, and no postal or telegraph services. During the reign of the Emperor Meiji (1867–1912) young Japanese were sent to study abroad, and Western methods and machinery were introduced. Great Britain helped build railways, foundries and cotton mills; the United States started educational and postal services; the French drew up a criminal code; Germany trained doctors and officers for the armed forces; and Italy introduced new ideas of art and architecture.

The Second World War brought the tragedies of the Japanese attack on the American fleet at Pearl Harbor, and the American atomic bombing of Hiroshima and Nagasaki. After the war the Japanese once again had to rebuild their country. Today Japan is one of the most advanced industrial countries in the world.

The Ginza,
Tokyo's
main street

Tokyo

In 1603 Ieyasu made Edo his provincial capital, but Kyoto remained the Imperial capital. In 1868 after the downfall of the Tokugawa *shogunate*, the Emperor Meiji decided that Edo, with its nearby port of Yokohama, would be more suitable for a capital than Kyoto. Edo (meaning estuary) was renamed Tokyo, or Eastern Capital.

Present-day Tokyo, with a population of over eleven million, is a sprawling jungle of concrete and steel. Milling crowds and the non-stop roar of traffic make it a tiring place to live in: rush-hour trains have special "pushers" to squeeze people into the already jam-packed compartments.

Much of Tokyo is very modern: there are superb elevated express-ways with tunnels and interchanges, a monorail from Haneda airport to downtown Tokyo, multi-storey car parks and huge department stores— some of them containing art galleries and theatres, roof gardens and base-ment steam baths. There are also many luxury hotels: on the sixteenth floor of one you can dine in a re-volving restaurant, with magnificent views of the city; in another you can sleep to the sound of recorded bird songs!

13

Olympic Games buildings designed by
Kenzo Tange

Although many buildings in
Tokyo resemble gigantic concrete boxes, others—including
those by Kenzo Tange, Japan's
leading modern architect—are
imaginatively designed.

There are skyscrapers of up to
thirty-six floors. The concrete
walls are pierced with vertical
slots, and six-sided cut-outs are
made in the floor beams—a new
engineering technique which en-
ables the buildings to ride an
earthquake or typhoon.

By the year 2000 the city's population may have increased to
thirty million. To meet this in-
crease parts of Tokyo are being
redeveloped into self-contained
districts. Low buildings will be
rebuilt into multi-storey blocks
with living quarters on top, and
each district will have a business
area, bus terminal, and an underground plaza with shops and
garages.

Amusements are many and
varied. There are golf driving
ranges, roof-tops netted for
basketball, baseball under arc
lights, indoor ski practice slopes,
and an indoor pool with a wave-
making device for surf riding.

Tokyo by night—the ventilation funnels
provide air for an underground plaza

14

Asakusa amusement district: choosing a
ticket for a lucky dip

As well as these Western amusements there are many places in
Tokyo which are completely
Japanese. The Asakusa amusement district is popular. Its covered streets are decorated with
plastic branches and yellow, pink
and blue lanterns. The stalls sell
everything from beanpaste sweets
and rice biscuits glazed in soy
sauce, to elaborate dolls and
ceremonial *kimono*.

Tokyo has many temples and
shrines. Yasukuni, with its high
stone and bronze archways, is
dedicated to all who died fighting
for their country. Meiji shrine,
which is in a beautiful park with
100,000 trees donated from all
over Japan, is dedicated to the
Emperor Meiji. Toshogu shrine,
in Tokyo's largest park (Ueno),
has an avenue of stone lanterns,
a five-storey pagoda, and a gilt
and red Chinese-style gateway
decorated with carved dragons.

Ueno Park also has a zoo and
aquarium linked by monorail,
the National Museum with its
great collection of Far Eastern
art, the National Science Museum, and a Festival Hall for
concerts.

Asakusa temple: worshippers rub their
bodies with incense smoke to purify
themselves

Akihabara

The Imperial Palace moat

Tokyo has many other parks and gardens besides Ueno. From the observation platforms of the Tokyo Tower in Shiba Park, you can sometimes see Fuji-san, over sixty miles away; and during the cherry-blossom season one of the most popular parks is the old Imperial Garden at Shinjuku on the western side of the city.

Tokyo's summer is very hot and humid. Patches of tar on the roads sometimes melt, unused clothes may become mildewed, and people carry little towels to wipe away the perspiration from their foreheads.

Although more and more buildings have air conditioning, many people have to make do with electric fans. When the hot weather arrives, Tokyo residents often go by subway to Akihabara. Its name means "the field of autumn leaves", but today this district is a maze of covered streets, with row upon row of small shops crammed to the ceilings with all kinds of electrical goods. The shopkeeper can sell his goods fairly cheaply—partly because he often buys cut-price bankrupt stock, and partly because he pays a low rent for his tiny shop and can sell his goods quickly.

In spite of Tokyo's modernization, there are still many residential areas both inside the city and in the suburbs, which have traditional Japanese-style houses and gardens.

ABOVE Tokyo old and new
RIGHT Kamakura—a popular beach with Tokyoites

To the east of the area facing the Imperial Palace, with its banks, government offices and Diet, there are still streets of old one-storey houses with wooden slatted window grills. These narrow alleys have a charm of their own—there are no gardens, but outside one house there may be cages of birds or tubs of flowering shrubs; outside another a glass tank or earthenware bowl of fish. In one street a man will be washing under a pump; in another, children playing in a plastic paddling pool. The smell of incense, of the fish market and pickle shops, and the smell from the Sumida river and its network of canals—this is just as much a part of Tokyo as the smart hotels and shops of the Ginza.

The Diet building: The Diet (Parliament) is made up of two chambers—the House of Councillors and the House of Representatives. The members are elected by the people—everyone over twenty has the right to vote. The Prime Minister is elected by the members of the Diet

Heian shrine: rinsing the mouth and hands to purify oneself before praying

Kyoto and Nara

The towns of Kyoto and Nara in central Honshu were once capitals of Japan—Nara for only a short period from 710 to 784, whereas Kyoto was the capital of the Emperors for more than ten centuries (794–1868). Its original name was Heian-kyo, Capital of Tranquillity.

Kyoto has magnificent palaces and gardens, and over 1700 Buddhist temples and Shinto shrines, many of them built hundreds of years ago. One of the most visited Buddhist

Primary schoolchildren in the gardens of Heian shrine—high school students go on week-long educational visits to places of interest

Hollyhock procession

temples is Kinkaku-ji—the Golden Pavilion—a 1955 reconstruction of the fourteenth century original. The most famous Shinto shrine is Heian, with vermilion pillars and curved roofs. It was built in 1895 to commemorate the 1100th anniversary of the founding of Kyoto by the Emperor Kammu.

Kyoto is a city of pageants and festivals. During the festival of May 15 when hollyhocks are offered to the gods of two Shinto shrines, horsemen and halberdiers in ancient court dress parade through the streets escorting the sacred ox-drawn cart. The Gion festival in the middle of July is one of the biggest in Japan. It began over a thousand years ago, as a means of asking the gods for protection against a plague which raged in the city.

Kyoto's gardens are world famous. One of the best known is the seventeenth century garden attached to Katsura Imperial Palace—a palace which was built for an Imperial prince. Katsura garden has flowering shrubs, lakes, and streams crossed by stepping stones and little humpbacked bridges. The moss garden of Saiho-ji is carpeted with more than a hundred kinds of moss. ("Ji" at the end of a word means Buddhist temple.)

Other temple gardens such as those of Ryoan-ji and Ginkaku-ji are made of sand. (The fifteenth century Ginkaku-ji, or Silver Pavilion, was named because the *shogun* had intended to cover the outside with silver leaf.) The sand garden of Ginkaku-ji is raked into a pattern of ripples to represent a lake in China.

A Kyoto garden

Kyoto and Nara have many art treasures. Some are in the museums; others in the temples and shrines. The medieval hall of Sanjusangendo in Kyoto contains a gilded wooden statue of the Goddess of Mercy over eleven feet in height, as well as 1000 life-size images of the same goddess. Another temple, Koryu-ji, has a beautiful wooden image of a meditating Buddhist saint carved over a thousand years ago.

Nara was built at the beginning of the eighth century, soon after Buddhism first reached Japan. The people showed their delight in the new religion by building groups of temples, painting pictures and making statues of Buddha. Some of these statues are of bronze; others of lacquered or gilded wood. But to the hordes of children who visit the town every year on school excursions, Nara means one statue above all others. This is the *Daibutsu*, a colossal Buddha over fifty feet high, which is said to be the largest bronze statue in the world.

An outdoor public telephone

Screen
painting

Many rooms have sliding doors, called *fusuma*, between them. Some of the finest are in palaces and temples, particularly in Kyoto. In Nijo castle the *fusuma* are decorated with white herons and long-tailed pheasants, and sprigs of cherry blossom on a golden background. There are snow-covered fir trees and tigers roaming in groves of bamboo (the painters had never seen living tigers or leopards, but they imagined the animals from skins brought over from the Asian mainland).

Kyoto is the most important district in Japan for the dyeing and weaving of silk materials. Many of the traditional goods produced here are similar to those made in the town for hundreds of years. These include china and lacquer ware, woodblock prints and fans. There are also many modern factories.

When a shop changes ownership or a new shop is opened, wreaths of plastic flowers are placed outside

Life in the Towns

Most of Japan's industrial towns stretch in an almost continuous line from Tokyo to Yokohama, through the port of Nagoya (Japan's third largest city), and from Osaka to Kobe. Although the country-side of Japan is so beautiful, the industrial "corridors" between the mountains and the sea are very ugly. Expressways with toll gates link some of the main cities, and this part of the Honshu plain is criss-crossed by electricity pylons and telephone wires, with the sky-line a mixture of smoking chimneys and concrete blocks of apartments sprouting television aerials.

The little streets of the bustling towns are more interesting than the main thorough-fares. Wayside stalls sell hot eggs, maize cobs or chestnuts, and the "shoeshine" man sitting cross-legged by the kerb will even fit a new sole. For many Japanese their work-shop is their home. They work in little *tatami* (matting) covered rooms opening on to the streets, a television set at their side. The people are hard-working, and the back-street shops, the home laundry and the hairdresser may be open until nine at night.

A lacquer worker—the floor is covered with *tatami* (matting) made of rice straw and rushes

As most of the houses have no numbers, and only the main streets are named, finding one's way about is difficult. Some people have cards with a map of their house and area to help visitors find the way, and in each district there is a plan of the houses with the names of all the householders. Even so, taxi drivers (and residents!) often get lost.

The towns are very noisy—there is the honking of horns and clatter of trams (streetcars), the clickety clack of *geta* (wooden clogs), the singsong cries of street vendors, and the blaring of transistor radios and juke boxes.

The towns are at their quietest on Sundays. In summer, the thousands who in winter left for the mountains with skates and skis, now go off laden with an assortment of equipment—cameras and sketching blocks, sports gear and musical instruments. The children carry fishing lines and plastic bags to hold their catch, or butterfly nets and small cages for trapping insects such as fireflies and crickets.

The old lady is wearing *geta* and carries her packages in a cloth square known as a *furoshiki*. When not in use this is tucked away inside the *obi* (sash which holds the *kimono* together)

24

The Inland Sea

Himeji Castle

Between the islands of Honshu, Shikoku and Kyushu, there is the Inland Sea, formed in prehistoric times by a fall in the land which caused the sea to flow in. Along its shores there are many ancient castle-towns. Some of them, such as Osaka and the port of Kobe have developed into commercial and industrial cities. The industrial district from Osaka to Kobe is a twenty-mile stretch of houses and factories, steel mills and shipbuilding yards. Japan's coinage is minted here, and there are many cotton factories.

Among the many cities on the Honshu side of the Inland Sea there is Himeji, which has the finest feudal castle in the country, and Okayama, famous throughout Japan for its eighteenth century garden. Shimonoseki, on the southwestern tip of Honshu, is connected with the island of Kyushu by two undersea tunnels—a railway and a highway.

25

The Inland Sea has hundreds of offshore islets, many of them crowned with gnarled and windswept pines. Steep headlands jut into the sea, and craggy, pine-clad cliffs with strange rock formations of caverns and natural bridges alternate with sandy bays surrounded by fishing villages.

The Inland Sea districts, sandwiched between two mountain ranges, are hot in summer. Early vegetables, fruit and flowers are sent from here all over Japan.

In the ten prefectures* surrounding the Inland Sea new industrial towns are being built. At Sakaide, on the north coast of Shikoku, there is one of the world's biggest ship-building yards, and many of the towns have textile mills, chemical plants and iron foundries. There are also large salt fields.

* A prefecture is similar to a state or county.

Salt fields

Some of Shikoku's smaller industries have been carried on for hundreds of years. These include lumbering, *geta* manufacturing, the making of paper parasols and kites, stone quarrying, and the seasoning and splitting of bamboo. Tokushima is famous for string marionettes, Marugame for *uchiwa* (the non-folding type of Japanese fan), and Matsuyama for hand-thrown pottery.

Ferry boats and hydrofoils provide transport to the coastal towns and villages. There are ropeways to mountain look-out points, and in summer visitors make pilgrimages to the innumerable temples and shrines. One of the most beautiful of these is on the island of Miyajima, where a Shinto shrine is dedicated to a guardian deity of the sea (photograph, page 6).

Restaurant at a mountain look-out point

27

The cultured pearl industry: after a bead has been put in each oyster they are placed in wire baskets and hung underneath rafts. Pearls are formed around the beads in about three years

On Honshu, fifteen miles across the Inland Sea from Miyajima, is the town of Hiroshima, a large part of which was destroyed by the first atom bomb.

Here is a Japanese account of the bombing:

"On the morning of August 6th 1945 the weather was fine and calm. Suddenly, at 8.15 a.m. an atomic bomb exploded over the city. The bomb fell rapidly with a trail of thick red columns of flame in its wake, and 42 seconds later at the height of about 1800 feet above ground level, it exploded with a terrific detonation in a fireball about 180 feet in diameter. The temperature of this fireball—often referred to as a miniature sun—is estimated at 300,000° centigrade. . . . In the raindrops there was much soot which was sticky as though oil had been dropped, but it had no smell and was quite different from oil. White clothes were spattered, and there were black spots on tombstones and leaves. The river water was black like ink. In the mud of the river radioactivity was strong. Carp, goby and eels were killed. Two hours after the explosion, fires broke out all over the middle of the city."

In the Peace Memorial Museum there are reminders of this city that in a moment had more than 200,000 of its inhabitants killed or injured: a blackened watch, a child's lunchbox, a mass of bones fused to molten roof tiles. The heat from the

RIGHT Praying at the cenotaph on the anniversary of the bomb

BELOW The Children's Statue. The ruined dome, blasted by the atomic bomb, has been preserved as a memorial

radioactive rays was so intense that money in a cash box inside a safe was burned beyond recognition, and over a mile away from where the bomb was dropped, the rays burnt through uniforms so that only the canvas backing remained.

The middle of the city was an atomic desert. Rocks and stones exposed to direct radioactive rays changed their chemical composition: roof tiles became bubbly like pumice, clay was carbonized, and rocks formed layers of new minerals.

Hiroshima has been re-built into a pleasant modern town. There are new bridges over the many river deltas on which the city is situated, and a Peace Park has been laid out. The park has a cenotaph designed by Kenzo Tange, and a statue dedicated to the memory of the children who died as a result of the atom bomb.

Kyushu

Kyushu is the southernmost of the four main islands. It has industrial districts with steelworks, coal mines and hydro-electric plants; rugged tree-covered mountains and valleys; active volcanoes and hot springs, grassy capes inhabited by monkeys and herds of wild horses, offshore pearl oyster beds, and roads lined with avenues of palms. Much of the vegetation is subtropical and in early summer the cactus groves are a mass of yellow blooms.

Beppu, on the northeast coast, is the island's most important hot-spring town. Many of the geysers, ponds and springs have a temperature of over 200°F (93°C). One pond—nicknamed "Blood Hell" is vermilion-red from the iron oxide in the clay; alligators and crocodiles are kept in another. In Beppu you can boil an egg in a spring in your back garden, and have hot mineral water piped to your house.

Mount Aso, to the south and west of Beppu, has five volcanic craters, and one of them—Mount Nakadake—is still active. The long steep slopes leading to the rims are covered with red volcanic rock and dusty, burnt out cinders.

There are continual underground rumblings from Nakadake, and fumes from the sulphur smoke catch at the throat and make the eyes water. Huts have been built near the crater to provide shelter if there is a sudden eruption of hot cinders. Many of the non-active craters have filled with rainwater, and in winter the Japanese skate on some of these crater lakes.

In the mountainous districts of Kyushu, Late Stone Age and Iron Age pottery and other articles have been found. During the Iron Age (AD 250–552) the Japanese buried their dead in stone tombs which they covered with mounds of earth. There are thousands of these burial mounds throughout Japan—mostly in Kyushu, Shikoku and southern Honshu, but as they are overgrown it is difficult to distinguish them from natural hills. Large numbers of *haniwa* (clay images) have been found on these sites. The *haniwa* may have been pushed into the terraces surrounding the burial mounds in order to stop thieves from disturbing the sacred tombs.

This modern bridge is the last of five which takes a road from western Kyushu across a group of offshore islets

Model of a *haniwa*

31

Western thought and ideas were first introduced into Japan through Kyushu. In 1549 Francisco Xavier, a Spanish Jesuit missionary, landed at Kagoshima and stayed there for nearly a year preaching Christianity.

Later the Christians were persecuted, and from 1638 until 1873 Christianity was forbidden. However, many Christians practised their faith in secret, scratching crosses on boulders, and attaching crucifixes to images of the Buddhist Goddess of Mercy.

Nagasaki, on the west coast of Kyushu, was the second city to be atom-bombed during the Second World War. Today Nagasaki has many industries, including shipbuilding and the making of electrical machinery. The shipyards build some of the world's largest tankers —giant ships of over 200,000 tons.

Many western and Chinese ideas reached Japan through Nagasaki, which is nearer to China than it is to Tokyo, and which was the only port left open during the 200 years when Japan was closed to the world.

A Nagasaki shipyard

Volcanic crater of Mt. Sakurajima —once an island in the bay opposite Kagoshima, Sakurajima has been joined to Kyushu by a flow of lava from the volcano

After Japan had opened her ports, representatives from many countries came to Kyushu. British engineers introduced machinery for cotton-spinning, and shipyards and coal mines were developed. Today there is an important industrial district stretching from Nagasaki and along the north coast to Kitakyushu, a vast city whose industries include iron and steel mills, cement factories and textile plants. Japan's largest coal mines are to the south of Kitakyushu. There are also mines which tunnel under the sea, with wind tunnels on man-made islands to give them air.

**A service at a
Shinto shrine**

Religion
and
Festivals

More than half the Japanese are Buddhists, and many of them also believe in *Shintoism*. (Shintoism, or the "way of the gods", goes back hundreds of years to when the first settlers worshipped spirits, in the belief that they would protect them from invaders and bring them luck.) They may have a Shinto wedding and a Buddhist funeral ceremony. Some homes have a Buddhist altar as well as a "god shelf", on which foods such as rice cakes are placed as an offering for the Shinto deity.

About eight million Shinto gods are worshipped, and there are gods of birds, trees, mountains, streams, wind and rain, industries, rice, silk culture . . . The most important is Amaterasu, the Sun Goddess. Her shrine is at Ise, a city on Honshu. The famous shrines at Nikko, north of Tokyo, are dedicated to the *shogun* Ieyasu Tokugawa. There are gold-lacquered sliding doors dividing some of the rooms and richly carved gateways decorated with dragons, gilded Pekinese dogs and red-painted demon kings.

Every shrine has a metal or stone trough full of water, and to purify oneself before praying, it is the custom to wash the

A Buddhist funeral ceremony

hands and rinse out the mouth. After bowing deeply in front of the shrine, the Japanese ring a gong or clap twice. This is said to call the attention of the shrine god to their prayers.

Many shrines and temples are built on mountain tops reached by hundreds of steps, or by walking up a steep mountain pass. The believers feel that by making a difficult journey their prayers will be answered. Old and sick people are often carried in litters.

Although some of those who climb Fuji-san are pilgrims, the majority are holidaymakers enjoying a summer vacation. Some tourists go part of the way by bus; others climb all the way, staying overnight in simple shelters. The paths are well worn, and during a summer weekend when several thousand want to reach the summit in the hope of seeing the sunrise, you have to climb in one long queue. Many people hike throughout the night carrying flashlights. At the top, there is a collection of huts containing a post office, a police box, and stalls selling food and souvenirs.

35

New Year's visit to Meiji Shrine, Tokyo. Most Japanese wear *kimono* only on special occasions or for relaxing at home

Although only about three quarters of a million Japanese are Christians, the Christmas season is becoming more popular. Shops in the towns are decorated, and some homes and schools have Christmas trees.

New Year is the most important festival, and on New Year's Eve many people visit Buddhist temples, where bells are rung to get rid of evil spirits. On New Year's Day most families put on their best clothes, visit friends and relations, and exchange gifts. On January 2 children practise the first calligraphy (brush and ink writing) of the New Year— either at home or in school. This is also the season when boys fly kites, and girls play shuttlecock and battledore.

The Japanese enjoy festivals, and every year there are hundreds throughout the country, many of them connected with Buddhism or Shintoism. On November 15 most families keep the festival of Seven-Five-Three. It is believed that these are lucky numbers, and so all children of three years, boys of five, and girls of seven are taken to a Shinto shrine, where prayers are said for their health and future happiness.

Gion Festival, Kyoto. The huge four-wheeled floats are typical of Japanese festivals

Japan is famous for its beautiful dolls, and most families have a collection superbly dressed in silks and brocades. These dolls are too valuable to be played with every day, but on the Girls' Festival of March 3, Japanese girls display them on shelves, and invite their friends to see them. Fifteen dolls make up the set: at the top there is the emperor and empress, and below them, three ladies-in-waiting, five musicians, two pages and three guards. The dolls are allowed to remain on view until the end of the month, when they are packed away until the following year.

May 5 is the Boys' Festival. A bamboo pole is fixed outside every house where there is a boy, and a cloth streamer in the shape of a carp flown from it (one for every boy). This fish is chosen because it is strong and courageous, and parents hope that their sons will develop similar qualities. During this month *samurai* dolls are on display at home, and copies of the coat of mail worn by *samurai* warriors of feudal days.

The People and their Homes

A house in the country—the cloth streamers have been flying for the Boys' Festival

More than half the country is forested, so the traditional Japanese house is built mainly of wood. Sometimes the outer walls are of natural, unpainted wood; sometimes they are of thinly split bamboo woven into a lattice. This lattice is then covered with a mixture of clay and chopped straw to which a layer of plaster paint is usually added. Many roofs are tiled, but in country districts rice thatch may be used.

The Japanese like their homes to have a feeling of quiet, with no bright paint. The rooms open into each other and are divided by sliding partitions, the wooden frameworks covered by white paper or glass sections.

There are two kinds of sliding partitions: *shoji*, which act as doors and windows and through which a soft light filters, and *fusuma*, which are covered with thick paper.

This arrangement of sliding doors is ideal for hot weather, but makes it difficult to warm houses in winter. Gas, electric and kerosene stoves are the main forms of heating. A traditional way of keeping warm is to use a *kotatsu*—a sunken hearth in the middle of the floor in which sticks of charcoal are burnt. The table, covered with a thick cloth, is placed over it, and to keep warm you tuck your feet beneath the cloth. Its modern counterpart is a table with an electric heater built in underneath.

Most Japanese-style rooms have a *tokonoma*, or alcove, in which there may be a flower arrangement and perhaps some household treasure such as a piece of pottery. The *tokonoma* also has a hanging scroll.

The Japanese prefer rooms uncluttered by furniture, but today's changing ways create problems. When people wore *kimono*, all clothing could be stored on shelves, but western-style clothes need hangers. Schoolchildren, and office and factory workers, have become used to chairs, and feel uncomfortable sitting for long periods on the floor. Chairs, wardrobes, clothes stands, television tables and many similar articles are becoming increasingly popular even in the traditional type of home. Nowadays many Japanese have a western-style room in their house.

Tokonoma

A Japanese home: in houses,
schools and hotels outdoor shoes
are left in an entrance hall

The floors are covered with *tatami*—rectangular mats woven from rush grass. At night the bedclothes are removed from a cupboard in the wall. One or two thin mattresses covered with a sheet are laid on the *tatami*, and quilts inside white covers put on top. The pillow is small and fat. Sometimes it is stuffed with feathers; sometimes—particularly in country districts— it is filled with dried beans, or husks such as those from rice.

The bedding goes back into the cupboard before breakfast, so that one room can be used for living, eating and sleeping. Cushions—kept in a cupboard, or in a neat pile in a corner of the room—take the place of chairs, and there is a low table for eating.

The Japanese are spotlessly clean, and nearly everyone has a daily bath. As the same water is used by all the family, it is the custom to sit on a little three-legged stool, and wash and rinse *outside* the bath. The bath is small and deep, so that you sit with your knees drawn up, the water reaching to your chin. It is a pleasant experience to relax in a Japanese bath, but as the people since babyhood have been used to very hot water —often over 110°F—the visitor is likely to come out lobster red! For those who have no bath of their own, every town has excellent public baths, with a communal bath for men, and one for women. Clothes are put in baskets in an adjoining room which sometimes has a raised *tatami*-covered platform where young babies can be left while their mothers bathe. The dressing rooms have hair driers and electrically-operated massage machines. On summer evenings many people leave the bath houses dressed in night clothes ready for bed.

A family meal: the parents are drinking *sake* (rice wine)

In many ways Japan is a nation of contrasts. Ice-cream and other foods are made and kept in hygienic conditions; the water is safe to drink; and people preparing and serving food (and people with colds) often wear face masks to prevent germs from spreading. On the other hand many houses have no access to sewers; some of the side-street shops burn their rubbish in incinerators on the pavement; and beside many of the roads there are open drains which smell in the summer heat. The Japanese know these shortcomings and are doing their best to remedy them.

Over 1000 years ago, the Japanese copied the Chinese set of rules about what is right and wrong. Today many of these rules are unaltered. The family is very important, and no member must disgrace the family name. After the publication of senior high school and university results, there are often several suicides from amongst those who have failed their examinations.

The yellow flags are for schoolchildren to carry to stop traffic when they cross the road—crossings in towns have bins each side for the flags

The Japanese have a strong sense of duty and a great respect for old people. In the past the eldest son always brought his wife home to live with his parents, but today young married couples want to have a house of their own. However, as the Japanese have been brought up to put the family first, and personal happiness last, the children may give up their home and live with their parents when they become old, or have their parents to live with them.

The Japanese are also very polite, and rather shy—particularly the women. A Japanese girl when she laughs may put her hand in front of her mouth, as in the past it was considered impolite to show a row of white teeth. (In feudal days married women usually had their front teeth blackened.)

Before the Second World War the women of Japan had few rights: they could not inherit land; they had to marry the man chosen by their parents; and they were trained to be obedient, not thinking for themselves or making decisions. In 1946 women were given the vote, and although today they are elected to the Diet, and there are many women engineers, doctors and lawyers, men have been brought up to feel superior, and this tradition still lingers. A Japanese woman would feel uncomfortable if a man were to give her his seat in a bus, and although this, too, is changing, it is still the custom for husbands to go to dinners and social gatherings without their wives.

Practising judo

Kendo

Arts and Amusements

The Japanese take part in many sports, particularly golf, swimming, athletics, mountain climbing, skiing and skating. Baseball is very popular, and children practise wherever there is space—up a side alley or in the dusty yard of a Shinto shrine. In the big cities there are performances of a form of wrestling known as *sumo*. Only large, very fat men take part, and to keep up their weight they eat huge amounts of food. Many people practise judo, archery (using a very tall bow) and *kendo*—fencing with a long bamboo stick which is held in both hands. *Kendo* is a noisy sport as the clashing of the wooden swords is accompanied by bloodcurdling shrieks and grunts. Masks are worn, and special padded clothing.

44

In Osaka *Bunraku* (puppet) plays can be seen. The puppets, which are two-thirds lifesize, have three men to handle them. The chief puppeteer works the head and the right hand, a second man the legs, and a third the left hand.

Two other kinds of Japanese drama are *Kabuki* and *Noh*. Some of the stories are taken from legends and folk tales; others are about the characters of feudal times. The costumes are magnificent with gorgeously patterned old-style kimono worked in gold and silver silks, and wide, stiffly pleated trousers of brocade. Men take women's parts, speaking in high quavering voices, and wearing elaborate wigs decorated with combs and ornaments. In *Noh* plays masks hundreds of years old are sometimes worn (photograph, page 10).

All three kinds of drama have narrators who sit either on stage, or on a small platform at the side. These narrators chant in a special singsong way which needs much practice. There are many other things which make Japanese drama so exciting —the dancing in ancient court costume, and the high-pitched notes of eastern music. The musicians play flutes, *shamisens* (a three-stringed instrument something like a banjo), and drums. The knee drum is dried over a charcoal fire backstage so that the leather will make a hard sound when beaten.

The Japanese enjoy making gardens and arranging flowers. Flower arrangements are found everywhere—in buses, banks, offices and factories. Flower arranging first began in the Buddhist temples, and one of the present-day schools, Ikenobo, was founded by a sixteenth century priest. Many people grow dwarf trees only a few inches high—bamboo, pines, maples and tiny fruit trees complete with blossom and fruit. Some miniature pines are 1000 years old.

The tea ceremony is another of the ancient arts of Japan. In the bustle of modern life, the drinking of tea in a ceremonial way helps to make them feel calm and relaxed. Water is boiled over a charcoal brazier, and the slightly bitter powdered green tea is beaten with a bamboo whisk to make it frothy. Everything—from the bowl you drink out of, to the flower arrangement in the *tokonoma*, must be looked at and admired. Girls are taught the correct way of bowing when greeting guests, how to walk gracefully on formal occasions when in *kimono*, and how to sit back on their heels with a straight back. A full tea ceremony takes over two hours to perform. Many of the teachers are men, and no well-educated Japanese girl would get married without knowing something of the rules of the ceremony.

Origami (paper-folding) is a popular hobby

Children at School

Children have both a given name and a family name. A girl with the given name of Aki-ko (autumn child), will be called this only by the members of her family and close relations. Everyone else—including teachers and schoolfriends—will call her by her family name with the addition of *san*. If her family name were Kato, she would be called Kato-*san*. As *san* means Mr., Mrs. and Miss, both a girl and her brother will be addressed as Kato-*san*.

The Japanese have one of the highest standards of education anywhere in the world. Schooling begins at six and is compulsory until fifteen. At primary school, which the children attend until twelve, great importance is paid to the Japanese language, science, mathematics, music, handicrafts and physical education. Outdoor sketching and painting classes are a regular part of the curriculum (see the cover photograph).

In Japan most primary school-children wear yellow hats like those worn by the children in the cover photograph. In wet weather, many children also have yellow raincoats, gum-boots and umbrellas. This makes it easier for drivers to see them.

Schoolchildren in northern Japan—this part of the country has heavy snowfalls in winter

Using an abacus for counting—abacuses are used in many shops and offices

Compulsory education at the junior high school ends at fifteen; over 70 per cent of young people go on to a senior high school until they are eighteen. One pupil in six attends a college or university.

The new school year begins in April, and during the term before, there are stiff examinations for any child who wants to pass from the junior to the senior high school. Children often work too hard, and mothers who are over-anxious that their children shall do well in the examinations, have been nicknamed "education mamas".

Throughout their school life Japanese children spend much time on learning how to read and write the difficult Japanese language. By the end of their second year in the primary school, most children know the ninety-six characters called *katakana* and *hiragana* which represent sounds.

Here are the two *hiragana* sounds which make up the word "cat", *neko*: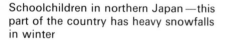

When they are nine, the children start learning another set of characters called *kanji*. *Kanji* look rather like pictures which show a meaning.

Kanji characters

man

tree

mountain

stream

48

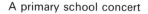
A primary school concert

Junior high school students practising
brush and ink writing—for everyday lessons a pen is used

By the end of their primary schooling, children are expected to be able to read and write 880 *kanji*. In the high school more characters are learnt. At one time there were as many as 5000 *kanji* in use, but nowadays the government has tried to simplify the language by reducing the number of *kanji* to about 1800 characters.

Japanese is read from top to bottom and from right to left across the page. Books are read "back to front" so that the beginning is where English ones end. During the fourth primary year, Roman letters (our alphabet) are taught. The Japanese have no "l" sound and find it difficult to distinguish between "l" and "r".

Tokyo station sign written in *hiragana*, *kanji* (Chinese characters), and Roman letters. Platform signs in Japan give the name of the immediate station, the last station and the one following

49

Farming

A hundred million mouths to feed, increasing by nearly a million a year, in an area approximately half the size of Texas or New South Wales—this is the problem continually in the minds of Japanese planners. The country, too, is so mountainous that only about one-sixth of the ground can be cultivated. Yet no one starves—in fact, the country grows more than three-fourths of the food it needs.

The farms are very small (an average of about $2\frac{1}{2}$ acres), but in the warmer parts two crops can be grown each year on the same land. Now that the Japanese are drinking more milk and eating more eggs and meat, some farmers are specializing in keeping animals. The country is heavily wooded, and except in the northern island of Hokkaido, there is little good grassland. The fertile lowlands must be used for rice-growing, not for pasture; often the cattle are fed on artificial foods and silage (hay and other green food preserved in an airtight building).

Rice, which produces more food per square yard than any other crop, is grown over half the arable land. Cultivation is possible throughout Japan except for the very north of Hokkaido. It is grown wherever there is land which can be easily irrigated from the rivers—on the plains, along narrow valleys between thickly wooded mountains, and on the lower terraces of the hillsides. Every year land is reclaimed for rice-growing: slag from ironworks is tipped into the sea, and in northeast Japan part of a lagoon has been drained and turned into paddy fields.

The Japanese countryside is very beautiful—particularly during the days of early summer. Against a background of mist-wreathed hills the land is a mosaic of different shades: melon clumps, rows of tobacco, and patches of spinach and eggplant, all provide a contrast to fields golden with ripening barley or white with daisies. Everywhere there is the vivid green of rice-seedling beds and the darker green of tea bushes. These mark the boundaries of the fields and provide farm-house hedges.

Workers in the paddy fields—the wooden tub contains cooked rice

Orange pickers

At the end of May, after the winter crops of wheat and barley have been dried and threshed, the fields are cultivated ready for the rice transplanting at the beginning of June. The rice is harvested at the end of September, and except in north Honshu and Hokkaido where it is too cold for winter crops, the land is replanted with wheat and barley.

The farmers grow many other crops including ginger and peppermint, soya and red beans. Rushes are grown for matting, and the paper mulberry tree for its bark which is used in the manufacture of hand-made paper. Crops such as sugar beet, apples and cherries are grown in the cooler northern regions, and sweet potatoes, oranges and peaches in the warmer south. Grapes, strawberries and persimmons can be grown over most of the country.

In two Honshu prefectures facing the Sea of Japan tulips are grown. In late spring a visit to the bulb fields is a popular outing with Japanese families. Farmers in other parts of the country grow flowers and shrubs such as cherries, wistarias and chrysanthemums. Some flowers are raised in the open fields; others in greenhouses or vinyl houses (bamboo-framed buildings covered with plastic sheeting).

RIGHT Cultivating paddy fields with a motorized hand-tiller

BELOW Sorting silkworm cocoons into sizes before sending them to the reeling factory

Cultivation methods are a mixture of old and new. Hoes and scythes, horse and ox-drawn cultivators can be seen in the fields side by side with threshing machines, insecticide sprayers and motorized hand-tillers. Some farmers take weekly jobs and look after their own farms on Sundays and holidays; others combine farming with fishing, forestry or sericulture (raising silkworms).

The most important silk-producing areas are round Kyoto and north and west of Tokyo. In spring, summer and autumn, the farmers sell the cocoons to the factories which reel them into silk. Silkworms feed on mulberry leaves, but scientists are trying to produce an artificial diet. This would be useful if the mulberry crop became diseased or if frost, flood or typhoons destroyed it.

On some farms silkworms are being raised in huts which are separate from the farmers' homes. This method is becoming popular with young farmers who do not like breeding silkworms in their houses.

Digging for shellfish

Fishing

As Japan has so many people to feed and so little farm land, she depends on food from the sea. Her yearly catch is the second biggest in the world and hundreds of different sea foods are eaten: fresh, dried, smoked and pickled. Sharks' fins and dried fish for soup-making, oysters and cuttlefish, giant prawns, eels cooked over charcoal, shrimps (sometimes made into sausages)—these are only a few of the fish foods the housewife can buy.

Each season has its speciality. In southern Japan from March to November small octopuses are sold from tanks on the quaysides. You take home your octopus in a muslin-covered jar filled with seawater, and boil it with sugar and soy sauce. (Soy sauce is a mixture of soya beans, powdered wheat or barley, salted water and malt.)

Winter and early spring is the season for raw oysters. Women working in sheds on the quaysides remove the oysters from the shells and put them in plastic bags for sale, or prepare them for smoking or canning in soy sauce.

An octopus seller

54

An Inland Sea
fishing village

In Hokkaido crabs caught off the coast are a winter delicacy. During December and January they are sold in the shops and on station platforms.

Much of the fish catch comes from the coastal waters. Some fishermen bring in fish such as cod, halibut, flatfish and herring; other catches include sardine, bonito (a fish of the mackerel family), swordfish and squid.

Japan has to guard against overfishing her coastal waters. Ways are being worked out to attract more fish into the seas round Japan. Some years ago an earthquake in northwestern Japan caused several blocks of flats to topple over. After the debris of the buildings had been tipped into the sea it was found that large numbers of fish had laid their eggs in these undersea "flats". So to encourage fish to breed, concrete tanks with open spaces in the sides have now been lowered on to the sea bed. These tanks have been named "fishes' heavens".

Unloading
frozen tuna,
Tokyo port

In the sheltered bays of the Inland Sea there are many fish farms
where eggs are hatched artificially, and the young fish are kept in
cages. When they are small they are fed on food such as sand eel
which is put through a giant mincer on the quayside. Many of the
hatcheries are so large that motor boats are used to spray the food
onto the water. Some fish are later released into the sea to restock it;
others are kept until they are big enough to eat, when they are
packed in dry ice and sent to different parts of the country. Red
sea bream, octopus, oysters, and prawns are bred in Inland Sea
hatcheries; salmon and trout in the rivers of Hokkaido.

Japan also exports fish. Salmon fishing boats leave for Alaska from
ports in Hokkaido. Other deep-sea fleets sail to the South Pacific
for tuna, and to the Antarctic for whales. The salmon, tuna and
whaling fleets have mother ships which are floating factories which
process, can and refrigerate the fish. The canned goods are often
transferred at sea to cargo boats and shipped directly overseas.
Great Britain, the United States and West Germany are the chief
markets for Japanese tuna and salmon.

56

Food and Drink

The Japanese enjoy both eastern and western food. They eat lots of salads, and tinned spaghetti with hamburgers and eggs is a popular dish in city snack bars. With this kind of meal knives and forks are used instead of chopsticks.

A *sushi* restaurant

Sushi restaurants are very popular. *Sushi* are rice balls sprinkled with vinegar and rolled in dried seaweed, or prepared with a slice of raw fish on top. Served like this—very fresh because it is caught and eaten the same day—raw fish is not unpleasant.

For a quick, cheap and filling lunch, the Japanese often go to a noodle restaurant. Noodles are made from dough cut into strips and cooked in boiling water.

Coffee, milk, fruit juices, yogurt and Coca-Cola are popular, and everyone drinks green tea. Japanese green tea is in fact a light yellowish brown, and has a slight, almost medicinal tang. It is very refreshing in hot weather and is drunk without milk or sugar. (For the tea ceremony a powdered green tea is used and this is a true shade of green.)

In Japan to make a sucking noise when drinking or eating is not thought bad manners, but usually shows that you appreciate the food.

57

In Japanese-style hotels meals are served in your room —the red lacquer bowl contains fish soup; the other bowl contains rice

In *sukiyaki* and *tempura* restaurants the food is cooked in pans over charcoal or electric braziers. For *tempura*, vegetables and pieces of fish—particularly fat, juicy prawns—are dipped in batter and fried in oil; *sukiyaki* is thinly sliced beef cooked in soy sauce with chopped vegetables and dipped into a raw egg before eating. *Sake* (rice wine) is often drunk with these dishes.

Many people in the cities eat bread once a day and rice at other meals. At the house where I stayed in Tokyo two breakfasts were cooked: the grandchildren had cereals, toast and coffee; the grandparents a traditional breakfast. In addition to rice this includes fish, and pickled vegetables such as cucumber, and slices of a giant radish which grows to over a foot in length. With a Japanese breakfast, a special soup is served. The housewife first prepares a fish stock with water and shredded dried bonito. She then adds fermented soya bean paste and a few pieces of seaweed.

Children enjoy eating ice cream and chocolates, as well as Japanese foods such as *gingko* nuts (they are small and taste something like chestnuts), and hot batter cakes sandwiched together with a sweet jam made from *azuki* (red beans).

58

Travelling at 130 mph between Tokyo and Osaka, the world's fastest train passes Fuji-san

Industry and Transport

During the past fifteen years Japanese industry has expanded rapidly so that today she is one of the world's leading industrial nations. She builds more and larger ships than any other country, and after the U.S.A. and U.S.S.R. is the world's biggest steel manufacturer.

Japan produces silk, paper and cultured pearls, but the country has very few minerals and nearly all the raw materials for industry have to be imported.

In the car industry as in other industries, the most up-to-date ideas are used—for example, the latest taxis have air conditioning and automatic doors controlled by the driver, and some have a device to purify the exhaust gas. One family in ten owns a car, and thousands of vehicles are taken on special two-storeyed freight trains to the ports for export.

One of the most important heavy industries is the manufacture of chemical products, including dynamite and fertilizers. Among other exports are clothing made from cotton and from man-made materials, toys, china and sewing machines, plywood and cement. The U.S.A. buys over a quarter of Japan's exports.

Some Japanese products

To make more land for industry around Kobe and in other places, the Japanese are bulldozing earth from the sides of hills and dumping it in the sea. This "sea building" is providing towns with new land for factories, oil refineries and housing estates.

59

Assembly line for transistor radios

The Japanese are an artistic people and they have always had a special ability for making dainty and beautiful things—woodcuts, lacquer work, hand-painted pottery and exquisite designs on silk. Today these things are still made, but the ability of first-class engineers has led to the development of an important electronics industry which makes everything from transistor radios to space communications equipment.

Nearly every Japanese family owns a television set, and three out of four have washing machines. As the people earn higher wages, goods such as electric rice-cookers and air conditioners are in great demand.

The Japanese are keen photographers, and at beauty spots all over the country they queue up to take a snap from the best viewpoint. Japanese factories produce some of the finest cameras in the world, and export them in large numbers to the U.S.A., Britain and elsewhere. Several million watches are also exported every year.

Throughout Japan dams store water for drinking and irrigation, and for generating power for industry. The country is developing atomic energy for peaceful purposes. There is one nuclear-powered electrical station and more are planned for the future.

Heavy electrical machinery

60

Growing industry needs a good transport system. Steam trains are disappearing, old lines are being electrified, and new ones built. With so much mountainous country and with so many small islands, it is not easy to build railways in Japan. There are plans to join Honshu and Shikoku with a railway bridge, and by 1975 the world's longest undersea railway tunnel ($13\frac{3}{4}$ miles) will link north Honshu with Hokkaido.

On the new roads there is a service of long-distance air-conditioned buses. Uniformed hostesses sing folk songs to the passengers, and give them information about the countryside.

By 1974 there will be a second Tokyo international airport on the eastern side of the city. Japan Air Lines (J.A.L.) is the country's largest airline, and the company has daily flights to different parts of Japan as well as flights to Europe, America and southeast Asia. Jets on a round-the-world service link Tokyo with San Francisco, New York and London, where connecting flights follow the ancient "Silk Road" to Japan—flying via Europe, Egypt, Iran, Pakistan, India, Thailand and Hongkong. Other jets fly from Europe over the North Pole to Anchorage in Alaska, and then non-stop to Tokyo.

J.A.L. is the first foreign airline to have a service across Siberia between Tokyo and Moscow (at the moment the aircraft used are Russian, and have joint Russian and Japanese markings).

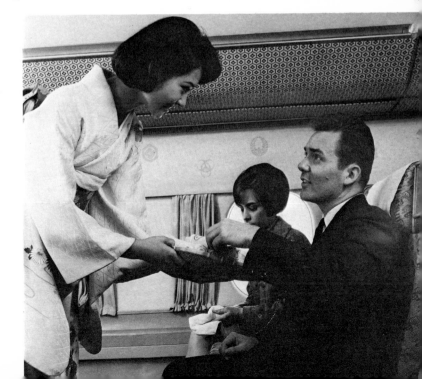

A Japan Air Lines hostess gives out hot towels for wiping the hands and face—in many homes and restaurants this custom takes place before meals

A dairy farm—
the towers contain silage

Hokkaido

The northern island of Hokkaido is about the same size as Scotland or the state of South Carolina. As there is snow for four months of the year, the houses are built of brick, concrete blocks, or clapboard (wooden planks covering the outside). Many of the houses have porches, double-glazed windows, and chimneys for coal or wood-burning stoves.

In the past Hokkaido was a "frontier province" and only the more adventurous settled there. Even today out of a total population of 100 million only 5 million live in Hokkaido. In the 1870's Sapporo, which was then just a small settlement, was laid out after the American style with wide tree-lined streets crossing each other at right angles. Sapporo is now the largest city north of Tokyo. It is a winter sports town with ski slopes in the nearby mountains.

Coal is mined in a number of places in Hokkaido, and about half the coal from the mines is sent to towns such as Yokohama and Kobe where it is used for industry.

The island has mountains, and vast forests of oak, beech, fir and pine, which provide the raw material for wood pulp and paper mills, and for factories making furniture and skis.

Fishing and farming are also important. There is pasture for dairy cows and sheep, and many crops grow well in the cooler climate.

Park in Sapporo

62

Ainu trout and maize seller

Many Japanese spend their summer holidays in Hokkaido in order to get away from the heat of Tokyo and the big cities. In the middle of the island there is Japan's largest National Park, Daisetsuzan (Great Snow Mountains).

In the lakes of Akan National Park to the east, a strange water plant known as *marimo* is found. The green moss balls take in oxygen from the water, float gradually to the surface where they release the gas, and then sink to the bottom again. *Marimo* is so rare that it is protected by law and must not be taken away.

In Hokkaido there are about 17,000 *Ainu*. The *Ainu* are the aborigines (earliest known inhabitants) of Japan. They are a different race from the Japanese, and nobody really knows where they came from originally. They may have journeyed from the part of Russia around the Black Sea. The *Ainu* have blue eyes, black hair and are powerfully built. They live mainly by fishing and farming, and by carving articles such as wooden bears for tourists. The *Ainu* are Japanese citizens, and although there is an *Ainu* language, today they all speak Japanese and there is very little difference in their manners and customs.

Japan has tremendous plans for the future: industries are growing, and new towns, roads and railways are being built. Larger quantities of food will be needed, and much of this will be grown on the now undeveloped lands of Japan's northernmost island.

63

Index